Sports Dictionary

Key:
- play outdoors
- play indoors
- play on your own
- play in a team

Written by Christine Butterworth

Archery

You shoot the arrow at the target.

Baseball

You hit the ball as far as you can, and run round the bases.

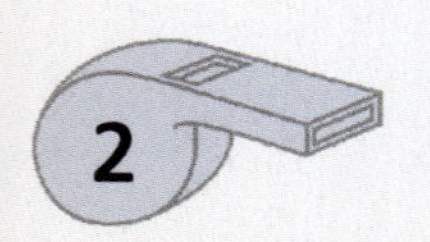

Basketball

You throw the ball through the hoop.

Canoeing

You use a paddle to row your canoe.

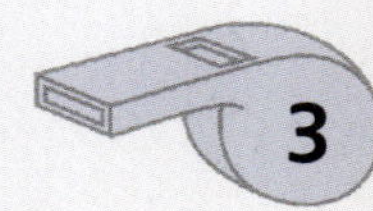

Cricket

You bowl the ball
or hit it with a bat.

Fishing

You use a net or a line
to catch your fish.

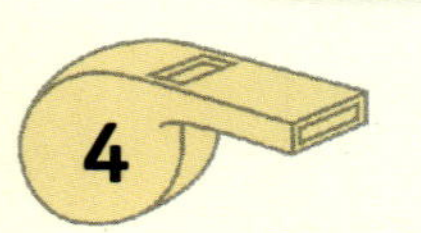

Football

You kick the ball
into the net
to score a goal.

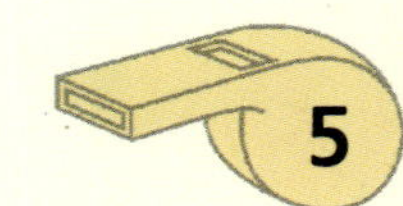

Ice hockey

You hit the puck into the net to score a goal.

net

puck

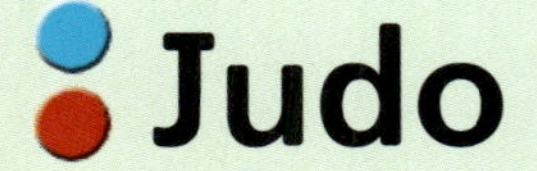

Judo

You throw the other person on the mat.

Kite flying

You fly your kite high in the air.

kite

sandpit

Long jump

You run up and jump as far as you can.

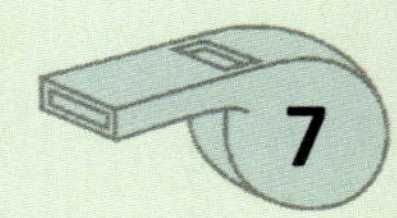

Motor racing

You drive fast round a track.

track

Quad biking

You can ride a quad bike over bumps.

quad bike

Rock climbing

You look for safe places to hold on.

climbing wall

Rowing

You use oars
to row a boat.

Show jumping

You ride a horse and
jump fences.

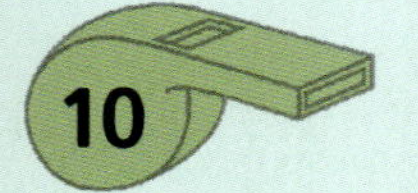

Tennis

You hit the ball over the net.

Volleyball

You keep the ball in the air all the time.

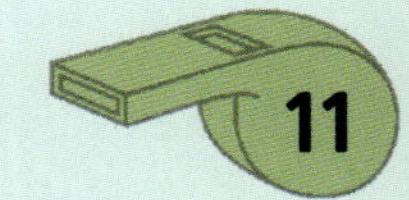

Wind surfing

You surf on a board
on the sea.

sail

board

sail

Yacht racing

You move the sail
to move the yacht.

yacht